MW01614906

Grace
FOR BEGINNERS

Mike Mazzalongo

THE "FOR BEGINNERS" SERIES

The "For Beginners" series of video classes and books provide a non technical and easy to understand presentation of Bible books and topics that are rich in information and application for the beginner as well as the mature Bible student.

For more information about these books, CDs and DVDs visit: **bibletalk.tv/for-beginners**

Copyright © 2014 by Mike Mazzalongo

ISBN: 978-0-9904155-6-5

BibleTalk Books
14998 E. Reno
Choctaw, Oklahoma 73020

Scripture quotations taken from the New American Standard Bible®, Copyright © 1960, 1962, 1963, 1968, 1971, 1972, 1973, 1975, 1977, 1995 by The Lockman Foundation Used by permission. (www.Lockman.org)

TABLE OF CONTENTS

CHAPTER 1
WHAT'S SO GOOD ABOUT THE GOOD NEWS?

The hymn entitled, "Amazing Grace," is one of the best known hymns sung by believers and unbelievers alike as it describes the beauty of God's grace.

It is interesting that it is this concept of grace in the Christian religion that captures the imagination of people when they think about Christianity, and it is this idea so beautifully captured in this song.

Not many people realize that John Newton, who wrote this song, also wrote nine additional verses to the four that are usually printed in our songbooks. John Newton's life was an embodiment of this song. When he was seven years old he lost his mother. Later, he became a sailor and eventually worked on slave ships. In a cruel irony, he himself became a slave and was sold to a black woman who treated him like an animal as revenge for those who so badly treated her own people. He was saved from this degrading life and became a minister and writer of hymns that stirred the hearts of people the world over. Shortly before his death, in 1807, he wrote,

Though I am not what I ought to be, nor what I wish to be, nor what I hope to be; I can truly say that I am not what I once was, a slave to sin and Satan; and I can heartily join with the Apostle (Paul) and acknowledge, by the grace of God, I am what I am.

In this book I am going to try to describe this *amazing grace* that John Newton so powerfully felt and wrote about.

Grace is "AMAZING"

There are several ways of learning what the Bible says about a subject or a word. A first step is to begin with the original meaning of the word you are studying and then examine how Jesus and the Apostles used it.

The New Testament was first written in the Greek language and so the original Greek word translated into the English word "grace" was the word *CHARIS*. In early Greek literature the word *CHARA* from which *CHARIS* is taken meant beautiful, lovely, attractive, charming and that which is delightful. By New Testament times, the word had come to signify joy or rejoicing. In later Latin translations the word also included the idea of gratitude.

When all these ideas are combined, our word grace refers to that which is lovely, happy and generous (as in giving or receiving a gift). Grace is not itself a thing but rather a word that describes the nature and value of something else. In normal literature it is used to describe a spirit of generosity, kindness and loveliness (e.g. he is gracious, she is graceful).

In Biblical terms the word is used to describe God's attitude and actions towards mankind. What God has done for man, from the creation of the universe to the saving of his soul, is referred to as grace, God's grace.

The word Grace is used in a variety of ways in the New Testament. We find it 170 times in all and 101 times by

Paul the Apostle alone, but never once by Jesus because the Bible refers to Him as the epitome of grace.

> For the Law was given by Moses but grace and truth came by Jesus Christ.
>
> - John 1:17

Because "grace" is at once a simple yet vast subject, there are many misunderstandings concerning it.

The essential meaning of grace

Although the word grace can be used to describe God's essential character (kind, generous), God's attitude in creating the world (joyful) or how we should treat each other (mercifully), the most repeated and important idea that this word describes has to do with mankind's salvation from sin.

The basic doctrine of the Bible is the doctrine of salvation. The entire Bible has been produced in order to explain this one important idea. Of course in the process of doing this, God has also managed to describe how the world and mankind were created, how sin came into the world, how He created a special nation of people called the Jews and all other related information that tell us the story of Jesus, the early church and the eventual end of the world.

However, all of this revelation and information have been given in order to provide a backdrop and explanation for the most important thing He wanted to accomplish: saving mankind from destruction. This

✳salvation was motivated by His grace and accomplished through His grace. This is why the Bible calls it salvation by grace.

> For by grace you have been saved through faith; and that not of yourselves, it is the gift of God; not as a result of works, so that no one may boast.
>
> - Ephesians 2:8-9

Salvation by grace, therefore, is **the** essential doctrine of the Bible. It is the key idea. Salvation is what God did, grace is why and how He did it. This is why the study of grace is so important. It is the study of God's character and motivation in doing what He has done for us. When I will be using the term grace therefore, I will be referring to God's kindness, generosity and joyfulness, as well as His method of saving sinful man.

The danger of grace

Believe it or not, some people think grace or too much grace is dangerous. There are several reasons for this:

1. Some do not understand the idea in the first place.

They think that grace is liberty; that grace means the freedom to do what you want or that God excuses sin because of His goodness. We have a duty to reject liberalism hiding as grace but should not deny legitimate grace in the process.

2. Some prefer the "works" system.

Human pride prefers the "law." In the "law" system man can pay something or do something in order to achieve salvation. Things like living according to a high moral code, following strict ritual rules or offering personal sacrifice cost man something and feel religious but these things cannot be exchanged for forgiveness and perfection because they are themselves not perfect or enough. The grace system requires man to abandon all efforts of self salvation and this is difficult.

3. Some fear living by faith.

> and may be found in Him, not having a righteousness of my own derived from the Law, but that which is through faith in Christ, the righteousness which comes from God on the basis of faith, that I may know Him and the power of His resurrection and the fellowship of His sufferings, being conformed to His death; in order that I may attain to the resurrection from the dead.
>
> - Philippians 3:9-11

Grace requires that we totally depend on God for righteousness, and this offer sounds too good to be true so we want to "hedge our bets" with another method. We have to accept the fact that it is grace or nothing!

> I am amazed that you are so quickly deserting Him who called you by the grace of Christ, for a different gospel; which is really not another; only there are some who are disturbing you and want

to distort the gospel of Christ. But even if we, or an angel from heaven, should preach to you a gospel contrary to what we have preached to you, he is to be accursed!

- Galatians 1:6-8

We need to realize that the danger in the church that Paul was writing to was not that they were going in the direction of too much grace or cheap grace, but rather letting grace go and trading it in for a more comfortable and predictable system of law (you do this, you get that).

In order to avoid these mistakes we need to go back to the Apostles' teaching to the early church about the subject of grace.

The essential teaching

Now when they heard this, they were pierced to the heart, and said to Peter and the rest of the apostles, "Brethren, what shall we do?" Peter said to them, "Repent, and each of you be baptized in the name of Jesus Christ for the forgiveness of your sins; and you will receive the

gift of the Holy Spirit. For the promise is for you and your children and for all who are far off, as many as the Lord our God will call to Himself." And with many other words he solemnly testified and kept on exhorting them, saying, "Be saved from this perverse generation!" So then, those who had received his word were baptized; and that day there were added about three thousand souls. They were continually devoting themselves to the apostles' teaching and to fellowship, to the breaking of bread and to prayer.

- Acts 2:37-42

Question:
What doctrine was Luke referring to that the Apostles taught?

Answer:
The person and direct teachings of Christ. The book of Acts and the epistles were not written when this was happening.

Question:
What, exactly, would they be teaching to these people?

Answer:
Acts 5:28-32: the person of Christ; His teachings; the plan of salvation (God sends Christ) and the believer's response to God (repentance and baptism).

The Apostles taught that grace motivated God to save man through Jesus Christ.

For God so loved the world, that He gave His only begotten Son, that whoever believes in Him shall not perish, but have eternal life.

- John 3:16

We make a fundamental mistake when we begin teaching someone the gospel and we begin by teaching them church history and organization or the falseness of other religions or how to respond to the gospel (belief/repentance/confession/baptism) rather than the good news of the gospel which is the fact that we are saved by grace.

The first point I want to make about grace and salvation is this:

- We are saved through God's grace (kindness, mercy, love, generosity). This is the **motivation**, the nature of salvation.

- We are saved through faith in Jesus Christ. This is the **method** (as opposed to no salvation or salvation through works of law).

- We are saved through baptism (I Peter 3:21). This is the proper Biblical **demonstration** of faith (as opposed to responding by intellectual assent; crossing yourself; saying "I accept Jesus as my personal Savior"; speaking in tongues, etc.).

When it came to the Apostles' teaching concerning salvation, this is what they taught the early disciples:

- Saved through grace – John 3:16
- Saved through faith – Luke 8:12
- Saved through baptism – Mark 16:16

Jesus taught that one was saved in all three contexts. Our study will see how these ideas are linked together.

Grace is free

...but the free gift of God is eternal life through Jesus Christ.

- Romans 6:23

Paul is talking here about salvation being free, that God's grace towards us is free. What does that mean? "Grace is free?"

Now to the one who works, his wage is not credited as a favor, but as what is due. But to the one who does not work, but believes in Him who justifies the ungodly, his faith is credited as righteousness,"

- Romans 4:4-5

What does Paul say about the one who works and the one who believes? He says that the one who works gets what he has earned and the one who believes receives a gift.

In the book of Romans Paul uses the term "grace" to encompass not only God's love and mercy, but also the end result of that mercy, our salvation. So when he says grace is free, in a sense he is saying that God's love and kindness towards us is free, is a gift; he is also saying that the final result of that love and mercy (our salvation) is also free, is also a gift.

There is never a problem with God's attitude or His gift. The problem always lies with man and his understanding and attitude.

One idea that causes a problem with many is the idea that God's grace is free. Here is why they have a problem:

1. Free grace implies that man is totally helpless. If grace (God's kindness and man's ultimate salvation) is free, it means that man can do nothing to earn it (even if he wanted to).

Free grace eliminates "boot-strap" religion (pick yourself up); eliminates Christianity as a self-improvement course; takes away self-reliance (train yourself into salvation).

Free grace makes you dependent on God for everything and human pride does not like this. We do not know what it means to be totally dependent on God, and we usually do not want to learn.

2. Some fear the idea of free grace because they think it eliminates human responsibility. You can preach all you want about the five steps of salvation and what you must do to be saved without even mentioning grace and no one will say a thing. But do not preach free grace without mentioning human responsibility and obedience or else you will be labeled as a liberal or a heretic.

Are we more concerned about what a person knows concerning baptism or what they know about grace? Preaching grace does not eliminate preaching baptism but we need to remember the role of each.

- Preaching the grace of God is the message of the gospel, it is what is good about the good news.

- Preaching baptism becomes necessary when the hearer has understood and believed the good news.

Charles Hodge says, "Tell men what God did before you tell men what they should do."

The beauty and power of the gospel is that despite our sins, God chose to be kind and merciful towards us (grace) and He arranged for us to be forgiven and receive eternal life through no merit or effort of our own (grace).

Where does human responsibility fit in?

If grace is free (God's kindness and salvation), then where does repentance, baptism and faithfulness unto death fit in? If grace is free, then everyone in the world receives it and is saved, aren't they? If grace is free, why the daily struggle?

It's not what grace demands or requires. This is the way the LAW speaks. The law demands and the law requires (obedience, perfect performance).

Grace does not demand; grace produces, grace gives, grace motivates and grace provokes.

The Law demands perfect obedience and produces death because it shows you that you are imperfect, that you are incapable of being perfect and that the consequence of being imperfect is death. (Romans 3:20)

Grace demands nothing, requires nothing. It reveals God's awesome love in the cross of Jesus and in doing so it produces repentance, faith, obedience, joy, peace, etc.

> Or do you think lightly of the riches of His kindness and tolerance and patience, not knowing that the kindness of God leads you to repentance?
>
> - Romans 2:4

> But by the grace of God I am what I am, and His grace toward me did not prove vain; but I labored even more than all of them, yet not I, but the grace of God with me.
>
> - I Corinthians 15:10

Grace does not demand or require. It provokes, it produces, it creates in man all the things that lead to salvation. The things we actually do, from our initial confessing of Christ, to repentance and baptism, to the every day struggle with sin to live a Christian life is not a list of rules or works done in exchange for salvation. We do these things as a result of grace working in our hearts and minds.

LAW = HAVE TO
GRACE = WANT TO

And so, God's grace turns us from "have to" people to "want to" people (want to repent, want to be baptized, want to serve, give, do what is right, remain faithful). I become this kind of person because of grace.

The Law does not have this power, only grace, which is free, has the power to produce this in us.

Summary

So what is so good about the Good News? Because of His grace, God offers salvation and eternal life to everyone based on faith, not law or knowledge or culture. I will say it another way: God's grace makes it possible for all persons to go to heaven because they believe and not because they are perfect. As John Newton wrote long ago:

> "Through many dangers, toils and snares
> I have already come
> 'Tis grace hath brought me safe thus far
> And grace will lead me home"

CHAPTER 2
THE TRUE PLAN OF SALVATION

There are several ways to explain the following statement: "We are saved by grace through faith."

- Because of God's grace we are saved through a system of faith.

- Through God's kindness we are forgiven through faith in Jesus.

- God is so merciful that He offers us salvation based on our faith, not based on our ability to be perfect.

We believe this basic teaching of the Christian religion but we often try to change it into something else:

- God provides grace, we provide faith.

- God's grace is that He reveals what we must **do** in order to be saved (the plan of salvation).

- God's grace is based on our faith.

Many times our problem with grace is that we have a hard time understanding such a Godly concept and, as proud and sinful people, we cannot bring ourselves to accept **free** love and mercy. Usually we end up paying lip service to the idea of grace and reduce this core teaching of the gospel into a law/works system that is not biblical or biblically accurate.

For example:

A. God provides the grace, we provide the faith.

The idea here is that salvation is a prize inside of a safe and God provides one of the numbers of the combination (grace), and we provide the other (faith). Grace is God's responsibility, faith is man's. Each side contributes something to produce the final result which is salvation. There are two problems with this thinking;

1. We contribute nothing to salvation.

There is nothing we can do, not even the act of believing, that has any value in producing our salvation. If faith could in some way be counted as something we contributed, paid for or did to earn our forgiveness and salvation, then the question would be, "How much faith or what quality of faith is necessary to exchange for salvation?"

Faith is not something we give or exchange. Faith is the way we receive the free gift of salvation. God produced it through Jesus Christ and offers it absolutely free to those who receive or accept it by faith as opposed to earning it by law.

You cannot receive it by earning it; you cannot receive it by exchanging something for it; you cannot receive it because you deserve it; you cannot receive it through knowledge or culture or force or religiosity or magic. You can only receive it through faith in Jesus Christ.

2. This takes the glory away from Christ.

If, in some way, we could provide something (i.e. faith) to obtain our salvation, then part of the glory for salvation would belong to us. The whole point of God saving man by grace through faith is to reveal the glory of Jesus Christ and the love of the Father (John 3:16; Romans 3:21-31). However, because of pride, the human spirit refuses to be totally helpless and in need of undeserved mercy.

B. Grace is the revelation of the "plan of salvation."

Some believe that God shows His grace by revealing to us "how" to be saved (hear, believe, confess, repent, baptize). This formula is referred to as the "Plan of Salvation" and the revealing of this formula is what grace is.

I have said before that the biblical "plan of salvation" is that God saved man by grace through faith. This is God's plan to save man, these are the "...things into which the angels long to look" (I Peter 1:12), and "...the mystery which has been kept secret for long ages past." (Romans 16:25)

The mystery, the secret, the plan of God was that Jesus would die for the sins of mankind and that man would be saved through faith in Jesus Christ.

When we preach "the plan," the "5 steps," as the gospel, we are preaching salvation by knowledge; if you know and obey accurately the plan you will be saved. This approach says that God's grace is that He reveals this plan to us. This idea has its place in the preaching of the gospel but is not the gospel itself.

The good news (Gospel) is that because God is kind, He sent Jesus to pay the price of death for our sins and we can be forgiven of these by believing in Him. This is the good news, this is the plan!

This good news, this grace motivates one of two responses:

1. Disbelief, which is expressed in rejection of the message and a continued pursuit of the world.

2. Belief, which the Bible teaches is correctly expressed in the following ways - confession (of one's belief in Jesus as the son of God), repentance (turning away from sin), baptism (immersion in water) and faithful living.

Repentance, confession and baptism are visible ways believers express their faith in Jesus Christ. They are not the plan of salvation. They are not exchanged for salvation. They are the way one receives the salvation freely offered. If a person truly believes, the Bible (not the Church of Christ) says that his faith will be evident in an open acknowledgement of Jesus as the divine Son of God, a changed attitude towards sin, water baptism and a faithful (not perfect) life thereafter.

C. God's grace is based on our faith.

This idea suggests that our faith is in faith and not in Christ (I have confidence in my faith, its strength, its accuracy). But faith's power is determined by what faith believes. For example, if I believe that a tree is my God then my prayers, no matter how sincere, will not be answered because a tree has no power to answer prayers.

The power that saves us is Jesus Christ. He is the object of our faith. He is the one who saves. He accomplishes our salvation and answers our prayers because, as God, He has the power to do so.

It is not the strength of our faith, it is the object of our faith that makes the difference.

For example: Paul had religious knowledge, a miraculous appearance by Jesus, the full gospel preached to him by Ananias and he believed. So strong was his faith that immediately after he was baptized he began preaching Christ.

For example: The thief on the cross saw a crucified Jesus forgive His enemies and so he asked for that same forgiveness. He saw no miracles, no visions, he was irreligious; no one explained the gospel to him, he simply believed in Jesus.

Both of these men were equally saved, both are in heaven with God. Why? Because despite the difference in the quality, strength and knowledge of their faith: they both believed in Jesus. The **object** of their faith was the same! The result of their prayers were the same!

In this world, many people believe (accepting as true) in various philosophies and religions. The belief that leads to salvation, however, is the one where a person accepts as true the fact that Jesus Christ is the Son of God. That particular belief expressed in repentance and baptism saves your soul.

Do not envy another person's faith (i.e. knowledge or religiosity); do not be proud of your faith; remember that grace is extended to those who believe in Jesus.

Our faith is equal and equally saves us if we are focused on the right object: Jesus.

Grace and faith +

The elements of our salvation are God's grace and our faith but the Bible qualifies that these are not alone. Therefore...

A. Only by grace but not grace alone.

God's grace is His kindness and mercy; His generosity and love. Grace is God's character and attitude but it was not just His grace and attitude that saved us, this character and attitude motivated Him to **do** something.

Yes it is God's grace that saves us, but a grace that works to accomplish that salvation by: establishing the Jewish nation; sending Jesus; sending the Holy Spirit; sending the Apostles; sending the Church.

Only grace could and would work in this way to accomplish our salvation (pride would not do it; law would not do it; guilt or self-interest would not do it; compulsion would not do it)... only grace would and could accomplish salvation.

B. In the same way, only by faith but not faith alone.

The only way man can be saved is to accept this gift from God by faith. He cannot earn, deserve, exchange, know or serve God for it. Faith is the only channel by which the gift of forgiveness and eternal life are received. However, faith is a living thing, not just a concept; not just a thought.

If grace had not **acted**, man would not be saved. In the same way, if faith does not act, does not express itself, does not show itself to be true faith in Christ, it cannot receive salvation.

The very nature of grace is that it must **do** something (e.g. create, bless, save, etc.) if it does not then it is not grace.

The very nature of faith is that it must be **tested** (i.e. demonstrate its genuineness). It is not biblical, saving faith unless it strives to show itself to be genuine. The Bible describes the way that faith shows itself to be genuine, and how genuine faith actually blossoms. God does not demand that a rose seed become a rose, it is programmed to do this if properly planted. In the same way, if the seeds of Christian faith are planted in a believing heart they will produce repentance, acknowledgement of Christ as Lord, the willingness to be baptized, eagerness to follow Christ, the hatred of sin, the longing for heaven, the love of the church, the desire to know and obey the Word, etc. Faith produces these things naturally!

We are saved by grace (a grace that works to accomplish our salvation) through faith (a faith that demonstrates itself as genuine by what it produces).

Those who have a problem with grace

There is a danger that certain individuals in the church will refuse to accept grace on God's terms. There is also a danger of trying to accept Christ but not the grace He offers.

The Lord warns of these in His lessons:

1. Simon the Pharisee – Luke 7:36-50

> Now one of the Pharisees was requesting Him to
> dine with him, and He entered the Pharisee's
> house and reclined at the table. And there was a
> woman in the city who was a sinner; and when
> she learned that He was reclining at the table in
> the Pharisee's house, she brought an alabaster
> vial of perfume, and standing behind Him at His
> feet, weeping, she began to wet His feet with her
> tears, and kept wiping them with the hair of her
> head, and kissing His feet and anointing them
> with the perfume. Now when the Pharisee who
> had invited Him saw this, he said to himself, "If
> this man were a prophet He would know who and
> what sort of person this woman is who is
> touching Him, that she is a sinner.
>
> - Luke 7:36-39

What did Simon want from Jesus? He wanted to
associate with Him as a teacher, to hear Him preach, to
share in His popularity.

What did Simon not want? To give Jesus due respect;
to be in a position to need mercy; to offer grace to the
woman.

The Pharisees waited for a time to include Jesus into
their group of "teachers." After all, He was a dynamic
and popular teacher. What they did not want was to
need mercy or to be forced to offer mercy to others. If
you need mercy you have to be prepared to offer

mercy. Their hard hearts had become this way because they did not see the need for God's mercy for themselves and rarely had the impulse (the heart softening impulse) to offer mercy to others. Theirs was the sin of self-righteousness.

2. Jonah

The Jews of Jonah's time hated the Assyrians with good reason: the Assyrians had attacked them, they had to pay tribute to them and they were pagan idolaters.

Jonah was called by God to go and preach to the Ninevites (the capital city of the Assyrians). We know the story of his response and effort to run away. But the true story behind his effort to flee and not do God's will was evident: could not accept God's gracious attitude towards his enemy.

Jonah was happy to receive grace for himself but was not ready for God to extend it to someone else, and certainly not his enemies! For example:

1 – When he was first approached to go preach repentance to the Ninevites he ran away in order not to do God's will. In chapter 4:2, Jonah acknowledges why he did this: not because of laziness, disbelief or fear, he ran away because of God's grace. He knew that if they repented, God would forgive them and he did not want to be the instrument through which God's grace was offered to his (Jonah's) enemies.

2 – After he was swallowed by the fish and then released through God's mercy, he finally went and preached to the Ninevites. When they repented he was very angry – not at the Ninevites but at God.

Ninevites did not have to be circumcised; did not have to keep all the Jewish laws; did not have to pay back all the money they had taken from them; did not have to make up for all the harm that they did had caused Jonah's people. God simply forgave them because they believed the message and repented. Because of His grace they received forgiveness through faith.

Jonah was so upset that in chapter 4:8 he says, "Death is better to me than life." Jonah was angry because God was too good, too kind and too gracious to Jonah's enemies.

3. The hired workers – Matthew 20

"For the kingdom of heaven is like a landowner who went out early in the morning to hire laborers for his vineyard. When he had agreed with the laborers for a denarius for the day, he sent them into his vineyard. And he went out about the third hour and saw others standing idle in the market place; and to those he said, 'You also go into the vineyard, and whatever is right I will give you.' And so they went. Again he went out about the sixth and the ninth hour, and did the same thing. And about the eleventh hour he went out and found others standing around; and he said to them, 'Why have you been standing here idle all day long?' They said to him, 'Because no one hired us.' He said to them, 'You go into the vineyard too.'

"When evening came, the owner of the vineyard said to his foreman, 'Call the laborers and pay them their wages, beginning with the last group to the first.' When those hired about the eleventh hour came, each one received a denarius. When those hired first came, they thought that they would receive more; but each of them also received a denarius. When they received it, they grumbled at the landowner, saying, 'These last men have worked only one hour, and you have made them equal to us who have borne the burden and the scorching heat of the day.' But he answered and said to one of them, 'Friend, I am doing you no wrong; did you not agree with me for a denarius? Take what is yours and go, but I wish to give to this last man the same as to you. Is it not lawful for me to do what I wish with what is my own? Or is your eye envious because I am generous?' So the last shall be first, and the first last."

- Matthew 20:1-16

Note that the "all day" workers were all angry. Why? Do you think they had a valid reason to be so? Most people see this situation as unfair, however:

- No one was cheated. All received wages.
- The day workers received the agreed upon amount.
- It was no one's business or judgment how the boss spent his money.
- In the beginning the day workers were happy and eager to find work for fair pay in the first place.

What were they really angry about? They were upset by the boss's generosity. He seemed more generous to some than others.

They overlooked the fact that they had a generous boss who had been generous to them first and then to the others afterwards. Giving them work at fair pay when they had no work was generous. Giving others work at the last minute for the same pay was also generous.

We cannot accept a measure of generosity for ourselves and then complain if someone else is also a benefactor of the same person's generosity.

The day workers felt that they had "earned" their salary and wanted everyone else to earn it as well. Some Christians are like that because they think they have earned their way into God's grace. The Jews thought they had earned it as God's chosen people.

The late workers did not trust in their work, they trusted their boss to do the right thing and were rewarded for their trust, not their work.

The basis of grace is trust. God offers it to those who trust Him, not to those who think they have somehow earned it.

4. The Pharisee and the Publican – Luke 18

And He also told this parable to some people who trusted in themselves that they were righteous, and viewed others with contempt: "Two men went up into the temple to pray, one a Pharisee and the other a tax collector. The Pharisee stood and was praying this to himself: 'God, I thank You that I am not like other people: swindlers, unjust, adulterers, or even like this tax collector. I fast twice a week; I pay tithes of all that I get.' But the tax collector, standing some distance away, was even unwilling to lift up his eyes to heaven, but was beating his breast, saying, 'God, be merciful to me, the sinner!' I tell you, this man went to his house justified rather than the other; for everyone who exalts himself will be humbled, but he who humbles himself will be exalted.

- Luke 18:9-14

What is the difference between these two men when it comes to God's grace?

- The Pharisee thought he deserved it. The Publican needed it.

- The Pharisee did not want to need. The Publican did not want to die.

- The Pharisee never knew God. The Publican found peace in the arms of God's grace.

The Pharisee would have been upset if he could have known what God had done.

Answer this only in your own minds and to yourself: in all honesty, who are you most like, the Publican or the Pharisee?

The reality of the situation is that all of us are in the condition of the Publican whether we realize it or not.

Summary

We all have problems with grace from time to time:

- We have trouble forgiving ourselves and cannot accept that God will forgive us even if we do not want to forgive ourselves.

- We are angry when others who have hurt us find forgiveness from God while we are still harboring resentment towards them.

  o For example, I knew a woman who was upset at the thought that her husband, who had left her, could be forgiven and actually start a new life. She wanted him to suffer, not be forgiven.

- We have trouble with those who claim to be Christians but who may not agree with us on every point of doctrine. Of course some things can't be compromised.

  o For example, we cannot call a person a brother or sister in the Lord if they have not been saved by God's grace through faith in Jesus Christ.

However, there are those who refuse to allow God's grace to reach those who may have a different view of the "end times" than we do, or believers who worship differently than we do. Does grace cover moral failure only? What about failure in understanding or a legitimate and sincere difference of opinion?

I am not saying that we have to change what we believe is Biblical in the areas of morality or worship. I am simply saying that God's grace is for sinners. And all of us are sinners, including those who miss the mark on certain doctrinal issues.

The Pharisees were experts at discriminating against those who did not understand or practice all the minutia of the Law. Let's not be like that.

We can accept those that God accepts without approving of their errors. How else will we ever love and teach others if we do not extend the same grace to other people as Christ has so kindly extended to us?

Let us remember that every time we refuse to recognize and allow God's grace for someone else, we automatically stop the flow of God's grace for ourselves.

Let us also remember to preach the true plan of salvation so that we can encourage true and lasting conversions of those who are saved by grace through faith in Jesus Christ, not through works, perfectionism, knowledge, or effort.

CHAPTER 3
GOD'S MOST PRECIOUS GIFT

In this chapter we are going to look at the value of grace as a gift, but before we go on to that, I want to remind you of two important points:

1. We do what we do by the power of grace.

- Our obedience to the gospel (repent, confess, being baptized) is motivated or powered by grace.

- Our hunger and thirst for righteousness is powered by grace. We desire to be and do good because of grace, not because we want to earn our way into heaven.

- Our service, our giving, our ministries are fueled by grace.

Once we have seen and experienced God's grace in Christ, we cannot help but act in this way to one degree or another.

2. Grace existed in the Old Testament.

To say that people were saved by the Law in the Old Testament and we are saved by grace in the New Testament is incorrect. The Law was revealed in the Old Testament and was necessary to bring man to an understanding that he was a sinner.

However, it was God's grace that first chose the Jewish nation and gave them the Law. That same grace sent

Jesus and the Holy Spirit, established the church, preached the gospel and will resurrect the faithful in the end.

The Law is part of grace's plan. Without the Law we cannot appreciate the beauty and generosity of grace.

The people who were saved in the Old Testament were saved by grace through faith in the same way we are today. Their sins were sent forward to the cross for atonement and ours are sent back to the cross for the same atonement. They expressed their faith according to the teachings of Moses (circumcision, temple worship, food laws, etc.); we express our faith according to the teachings of Christ (baptism, worship, evangelism, etc.). They looked forward to the time when God would send a savior to save them from sin (their lives were based on the trust that He would one day do this); we look forward to the time when the savior will return and save us from the second death (our lives are based on the hope of our resurrection).

But from the very beginning, everything God did was based on grace, and all who were saved, before the cross or after the cross were saved by grace through faith.

> Behold, as for the proud one,
> His soul is not right within him;
> But the righteous will live by his faith.
>
> - Habakkuk 2:4

This has always been the method, this has always been the plan.

In the New Testament God revealed perfectly the plan and the person who would accomplish it, Jesus Christ. This is the main difference.

Grace as a gift

The New Testament mentions four main gifts from God:

1. The "gift" of the Holy Spirit

> Peter said to them, "Repent, and each of you be baptized in the name of Jesus Christ for the forgiveness of your sins; and you will receive the gift of the Holy Spirit."
>
> - Acts 2:38

The Holy Spirit given as a gift to indwell man and one day raise him from the dead.

> But if the Spirit of Him who raised Jesus from the dead dwells in you, He who raised Christ Jesus from the dead will also give life to your mortal bodies through His Spirit who dwells in you.
>
> - Romans 8:11

This is a gift because we cannot force the Holy Spirit to come to us, He is only given by God to those who obey the gospel.

2. The "gifts" that God gives to the church

Therefore it says,

> "When He ascended on high,
> He led captive a host of captives,
> And He gave gifts to men."
>
> (Now this expression, "He ascended," what does
> it mean except that He also had descended into
> the lower parts of the earth? He who descended
> is Himself also He who ascended far above all
> the heavens, so that He might fill all things.) And
> He gave some as apostles, and
> some as prophets, and some as evangelists, and
> some as pastors and teachers, for the equipping
> of the saints for the work of service, to the
> building up of the body of Christ;
>
> - Ephesians 4:8-12

God provides prophets, evangelists, teachers, elders to bless His church. These are gifts because God calls, equips and appoints these people to do their work in the church.

3. The Spiritual "gifts" the Holy Spirit gives to individuals in the church – Romans 12; I Corinthians 12

God provided miraculous gifts to some in the church in the beginning (healing, tongues, etc.) and continues to bless individuals with non-miraculous gifts today (serving, leading, teaching, etc.). These are gifts because God blesses the individuals with both the miraculous and non-miraculous abilities that each has.

4. The "gift" of grace

so that in the ages to come He might show the surpassing riches of His grace in kindness toward us in Christ Jesus.

- Ephesians 2:7

The embodiment of the gift of grace is Jesus Christ who accomplishes salvation for us. Grace (salvation through Christ, obtained by faith) is a gift because we cannot earn it nor do we deserve it.

The value of this gift

Sometimes you get a gift that you do not fully appreciate right away. For example, a bathrobe at first is not exciting or flashy but after it is broken in it gives many years of comfort. Grace is like that for many people. They do not fully appreciate grace until they mature in Christ and grow in understanding.

The gift of grace is the most valuable. Why? Because without it all the other gifts would not be possible. We could not receive the Holy Spirit, benefit from Apostles and elders or receive spiritual gifts without grace. This is why Paul refers to grace as the "...unspeakable gift."

Thanks be to God for His indescribable gift!

- II Corinthians 9:15

The expression of grace

We have mentioned that our faith becomes genuine when it is expressed in obedience, in service and in love. Faith must become visible and concrete to be viable. The fruit of faith justifies and confirms its existence. This is why James said,

> But someone may well say, "You have faith and I have works; show me your faith without the works, and I will show you my faith by my works."
>
> - James 2:18

Faith is only a concept until it comes to life and becomes real through a demonstration or a witness of faith. This is why we say that proper biblical expressions of faith are repentance, baptism, service, fidelity, purity, etc.

Grace is also only a concept until it becomes real through some form of expression. The consummate, final, full and perfect expression of God's grace in physical form is Jesus Christ. When we talk about grace, we are talking about Christ. When we are discussing the life and ministry of Christ, we are discussing the grace of God in action. In the same way, when we talk about good works, baptism, holy living, we are really talking about physical expressions of faith.

Paul expresses this idea in Ephesians 2:7 when he says that the riches of God's kindness find their perfect and final expressions in Jesus Christ.

What the gift gives us

When we receive a gift, many times the value or joy of that gift is based on what that gift does for us. For example, a money gift gives us the power to purchase what we desire. A music gift gives us the sensual pleasure of this art. A plaque or award gives us a sense of appreciation from others and the pride of achievement.

Each gift gives us unique things. In the same way the gift of grace does something for us that is wonderful and unique. Only this gift does the following things for us.

1. Grace produces our salvation

The problem with going to heaven is that we know how to go there but we cannot accomplish what is necessary. We know that if we are sinless, we automatically go to heaven.

> but from the tree of the knowledge of good and evil you shall not eat, for in the day that you eat from it you will surely die.
>
> - Genesis 2:17

Our problem is that even though we know that sin causes death and condemnation (Romans 6:23), we sin anyways. We are helpless victims of our weak flesh and condemned for it

> For what I am doing, I do not understand; for I am not practicing what I would like to do, but I am doing the very thing I hate.
>
> - Romans 7:15

God solves our problem by sending Jesus to live that perfect life in our stead and then offers it back to God as a payment for our imperfect lives. One perfect life offered for all imperfect lives.

God has solved our problem of sin and saved us from judgment, condemnation and eternal suffering. Now we have two ways to be saved: live a perfect life or receive a perfect life through faith in Christ.

God's grace/gift produces a new way to be saved which is available and possible for all.

2. Grace produces righteousness

One of the most unpleasant experiences we have as human beings is the knowledge and the feelings that accompany the fact that we are imperfect, impure and unholy. This knowledge of sinfulness and imperfection leads many to all kinds of warped behavior: some become depressed and insecure; others over-compensate and become proud, cynical or boastful; still others revel in their own evil and plug into its power to obtain their desires in this world.

The gift of grace/Christ, on the other hand, gives the individual "imputed righteousness" in order to satisfy that innate desire to be right with God and self.

There are different kinds of righteousness (being right, being acceptable to God).

- Inherent righteousness is what you have because it is your essential nature. It is what you are naturally. God has inherent righteousness.

- Achieved righteousness is the righteousness we earn or cultivate through willpower and training. This is the degree of goodness and acceptability we have through our own efforts and the conditioning we receive from parents. This is essentially a righteousness obtained through keeping the Law, a righteousness achieved by rule keeping.

- Imputed righteousness is the righteousness that someone else gives you. This is righteousness that God gives you through faith in Christ.

The righteousness (goodness or acceptability) that we need to be with God in heaven is His kind of righteousness. In other words, what is required is not inherent righteousness or achieved righteousness. We need Godly righteousness and we can only have this level of righteousness when it is imputed or given to us by Christ through faith. This is why people who may have a very high level of inherent and achieved righteousness that may even surpass that of Christians are not necessarily saved. They have righteousness but not the quality of righteousness required for salvation. That righteousness level can only be **imputed** by God Himself through Christ.

And so, the gift of grace is a great blessing because through it we receive the same Godly righteousness possessed by Christ Himself.

> For you are all sons of God through faith in Christ
> Jesus. For all of you who were baptized into
> Christ have clothed yourselves with Christ.
>
> - Galatians 3:26-27

No matter how much we try and train we could never achieve the same degree of righteousness through our own efforts as we receive freely and as a gift through faith in Christ.

This is why good people, moral people, nice people or kind people who do not have Christ are still lost. A person may have a high degree of personal integrity and rightness in his life, but these will never be able to substitute for the covering of Christ's own righteousness when he or she stands before God in judgment.

3. Grace produces life

We often think about grace in abstract or future terms only. Grace washes sins, grace produces righteousness, grace gives eternal life.

But grace is a gift for the here and now as well. It is a gift that blesses our daily lives. It is grace that motivates good works, perseverance, joy and obedience in our lives. Jesus said that He was the vine, we are the branches.

> You are already clean because of the word which
> I have spoken to you. Abide in Me, and I in you.

> As the branch cannot bear fruit of itself unless it abides in the vine, so neither can you unless you abide in Me.
>
> - John 15:3-4

This clearly teaches that those who are "in Christ," "in grace," will bear fruit. The vine feeds the branches and so the Lord feeds us, motivates us and enables us to do good works.

The good life we have, the holy life we aspire to, the struggle with sin, the personal spiritual victories, all of these find their original source in Christ/grace.

Do not be afraid that leaning on grace will cut your appetite for good or make you take things for granted. Grace has exactly the opposite effect. Eventually grace produces eternal life.

Falling from grace – Losing this precious gift.

What about the issue of losing grace? Let's get some background information first. There are some extreme positions taken when discussing this issue. For example:

1. Calvinism

In classic Calvinism the teaching is that there is no possibility of falling from grace. This idea has been set forth in 5 doctrinal statements.

The TULIP acrostic:

Total Depravity: Man is so lost and depraved he cannot respond to the gospel.

Unconditional Election: God, therefore, chooses some for salvation and some for damnation.

Limited Atonement: Jesus dies only for those God chose.

Irresistible Grace: Those God chooses cannot resist His calling of them.

Perseverance: Those who fall away from the faith are those who were never chosen to begin with.

These doctrines ultimately led to the position that once you were saved, you were always saved and could not be lost and that you could not lose the grace of God.

Of course a quick review of the Bible shows that this premise is unbiblical. Think now:

- Adam and Eve (perfectly created) were lost.
- Israel was lost (chosen by God).
- Judas was lost (chosen by Jesus).
- Demas was lost (chosen by Paul).

The book of Hebrews was written to warn people who were definitely saved, to be careful not to be lost!

For in the case of those who have once been enlightened and have tasted of the heavenly gift and have been made partakers of the Holy Spirit, and have tasted the good word of God and the powers of the age to come, and *then* have fallen away, it is impossible to renew them again to repentance since they again crucify to themselves the Son of God and put Him to open shame. (Hebrews 6:4-6)

So the Bible definitely teaches that it is possible for a person who is truly saved through faith by God's grace to then be truly lost. That includes you and me!

2. Pessimism

There is no one teacher of this particular doctrine but we, in the church of Christ, in an effort to confront and correct Calvinism may have gone too far and become pessimistic at times. Pessimism does not have any formal set of doctrines, it is more like an attitude that many possess in the church.

Pessimists do not only teach that it is possible to fall away, they teach that it is probable that apostasy will come and overreact to any effort at change in the church. The main error of Pessimists is that they misunderstand three ideas about grace:

A. The idea of falling from grace

Behold I, Paul, say to you that if you receive circumcision, Christ will be of no benefit to you. And I testify again to every man who receives circumcision, that he is under obligation to keep the whole Law. You have been severed from Christ, you who are seeking to be justified by law; you have fallen from grace. For we through the Spirit, by faith, are waiting for the hope of righteousness. For in Christ Jesus neither circumcision nor uncircumcision means anything, but faith working through love.

- Galatians 5:2-6

What does Paul say "falling from grace" is? We sometimes equate "falling from grace" to "falling into sin," which means that in order to remain in grace a person needs to be sinless.

Falling from grace is when you leave grace in order to go to a "works" system in order to save yourself. Do we think that perfect adherence to the rules of worship saves us? Do we think that proper understanding of the key concepts saves us?

Being in grace is the realization that your performance is very limited by sin and your knowledge is imperfect, but you are saved anyways because God's grace permits you to be saved through believing and trusting in Jesus, not perfect knowledge or rule keeping.

B. The idea that we create grace

So then, my beloved, just as you have always obeyed, not as in my presence only, but now much more in my absence, work out your salvation with fear and trembling; for it is God who is at work in you, both to will and to work for His good pleasure.

- Philippians 2:12-13

In other words, in order to remain in God's grace, we have to "work" at it. You have grace but unless you work (perform well) each day, God will remove it.

When Paul wrote this he was addressing a congregation that he had begun and led and loved but had not seen in a long time. He compliments them on their perseverance and good faith (even in his absence) and then gives them a word of encouragement.

1. Work out your salvation.

The verb means to finish or to complete. To complete the process that was begun in them at their conversion.

We are saved from judgment and condemnation but until Jesus returns we must preserve that salvation by remaining faithful (i.e. despite our sins, we continue to believe and follow Jesus). Finishing (or working out) salvation means to remain faithful. It does not mean that we must do something to earn or deserve what grace has freely given us. The key is to preserve not to deserve.

2. In fear and trembling.

We should not have fear or trembling of God because of punishment. We have been saved from that.

We should have fear and trembling of the evil seductions and the wicked plans of those who would try to destroy what we have. These words are meant as an encouragement to be on guard against those who would try to steal what is ours. Fear the devil, fear the world but do not fear God.

3. God is the one who wills and works.

If God is the one who wills and works within me, why should I "work out my salvation"?

Paul reassures them that despite the obstacles, despite the evil in the world and despite the weakness of our flesh, we possess God's Holy Spirit and have His inspired Word. Through these, God will guide our work and motivate our will so we can reach our goal.

Through God's grace we are not only saved, but that salvation is protected while we are still vulnerable to sin (while we still can fall) by God's Spirit and Word.

C. The idea that assurance leads to arrogance

> What shall we say then? Are we to continue in sin so that grace may increase? May it never be! How shall we who died to sin still live in it?
>
> - Romans 6:1-2

If someone sins more because he thinks grace covers his sins, that person does not understand the gospel and has never been touched by grace.

Assurance (confidence, peace, joy) is the primary fruit of grace, not arrogance (laziness, spiritual pride, immorality). Grace motivates love, service, piety and faithfulness.

Some think that it is arrogant to claim 100% certainty that they are saved and going to heaven. They think that not to be too sure about salvation is somehow being modest.

> I have fought the good fight, I have finished the course, I have kept the faith; in the future there is laid up for me the crown of righteousness, which the Lord, the righteous Judge, will award to me on that day; and not only to me, but also to all who have loved His appearing.
>
> - II Timothy 4:7-8

Note here that Paul is assured of his crown because he finished, he fought and he was faithful, not because he was perfect in knowledge or performance.

To be sure of salvation is the final goal of grace, it is what God wants His grace to do in our lives.

Summary

We need to see grace in the light of the gospel. It is not a commodity that we can buy or exchange. It is not a thing that we can earn or let slip out of our hands. Grace is like a relationship, it involves a relationship with God. It is a relationship with God based on faith, not perfection. For example:

- I am married. I am not a perfect husband, but I am a faithful one.

- I am a preacher. I am not an all-knowing preacher, but I am faithful to my calling.

- We are Christians. We are not sinless Christians, but we are faithful ones.

Because of grace, God allows us to have a relationship with Him based on our faith rather than our perfection. This is His precious gift to us.

CHAPTER 4
NO GRACE - NO GOSPEL

Many believers have an incorrect view of what grace means and does. In this chapter I'd like to review some of the more popular misconceptions about this important element of the Christian faith.

What grace is not:

1. Grace is not a dividing line

Some think that grace is a point that divides being safe from being lost. They reason that if they are on the safe side of the line, then they are under grace (grace begins at the line) and if they are on the other side of the line, they are out of grace and consequently lost. Many use this imagery to explain the meaning of I John 1:5-10.

> This is the message we have heard from Him
> and announce to you, that God is Light, and in
> Him there is no darkness at all. If we say that we
> have fellowship with Him and yet walk in the
> darkness, we lie and do not practice the truth; but
> if we walk in the Light as He Himself is in the
> Light, we have fellowship with one another, and
> the blood of Jesus His Son cleanses us from all
> sin.
>
> - I John 1:5-7

Walking in the light is being on the "grace side".

> If we say that we have no sin, we are deceiving
> ourselves and the truth is not in us. If we confess
> our sins, He is faithful and righteous to forgive us
> our sins and to cleanse us from all
> unrighteousness. If we say that we have not
> sinned, we make Him a liar and His word is not in
> us.
>
> - I John 1:8-10

If we follow this incorrect idea then when we sin we are on the wrong side of the line and need to confess sin and be restored to the "grace side."

The problem with this teaching is that we worry about being on the wrong side when death comes. When we see how weak we are and how easily we sin, it is easy to see how we could slip on to the "wrong" side even for a moment when we die... so we worry. We would worry less if we realized that John is talking about hypocrisy here and how God will judge hypocrisy. Not about lines.

If you profess to be a Christian, your life (walking in the light) will be evidence of this and the sins you commit while you are in fellowship with God will be forgiven you (vs. 7b) Notice the two situations are simultaneous.

Walking in the light is not being sinless. This expression refers to a relationship (walking) and an awareness (light). Walking in the light is the conscious relationship we have with God through our union with Christ expressed in repentance, baptism and fidelity. It is the ongoing **awareness** that because we are sinners we need Christ as our savior, we need His blood to wash us. This is why he says that to deny that we are sinners, and consequently have any need for Christ, makes us fools and liars.

John reminds us that we are sinners and always will be but so long as we are aware of this, acknowledge this and trust God for ongoing mercy, we will be saved: we are walking in the light.

Walking in the light does not mean we are sinless!!! It means we are enlightened about our situation.

2. Grace is not a thermometer

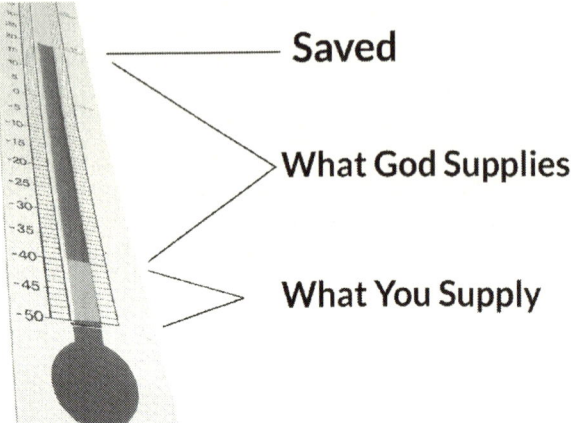

Saved

What God Supplies

What You Supply

I do not know where this idea comes from but it goes like this: in the process of salvation, you supply this much and God will supply the rest. Grace is the part that God supplies in the process of salvation. This imagery is based on the false premise that there is something that we supply in exchange for salvation and God, in His grace, supplies the rest.

When it comes to salvation, we provide **nothing**. Our role is to accept forgiveness through faith expressed in repentance and baptism. We do not exchange repentance and baptism for salvation, we merely express our faith this way.

> But by His doing you are in Christ Jesus, who became to us wisdom from God, and righteousness and sanctification, and redemption,
>
> - I Corinthians 1:30

Christ, on our behalf, becomes all that we need in order to be right with God; and we become right through our association with Christ. What happens at baptism is that our association with Christ begins and so also our advantages because of it; eternal life, Holy Spirit, righteousness, etc.

> and He Himself bore our sins in His body on the cross, so that we might die to sin and live to righteousness; for by His wounds you were healed.
>
> - I Peter 2:24

We often confuse repentance with restitution. The restitutionary (payment) element in our salvation was made by Christ. We contribute **nothing** towards it. Whatever way we sin, either before becoming a Christian or after, Jesus makes restitution to God with His cross. Some think that after baptism we have to make restitution for sin, but we do not see this example or teaching in the Bible.

We may have to make restitution to the government*, to a friend, to a spouse, but we cannot make restitution to God.

---

*Going to jail for stealing may make restitution to society for stealing, but our jail term counts for nothing as payment to God for our moral debt because of the sin of stealing. Only Christ can make moral restitution to God for our sins through the cross.

Repentance is a change of attitude about sin, about how we will conduct ourselves, about who and what we believe, but it is not restitution.

On the thermometer scale, Jesus supplies **all** of what we need to be saved. He makes 100% of the restitution with God. So, you stole? He makes restitution. You got an abortion? He makes restitution. You failed at marriage? He makes restitution. You abandoned the church? He makes restitution. This is the GOOD NEWS of the gospel!

3. Grace is not a free ticket

Some think that grace is a special privilege to sin without consequences. As if God is our buddy and allows us to enjoy ourselves in sin and lower standards of morality or ethics because we are His children and He (like earthly fathers) indulges us our weaknesses.

> What shall we say then? Are we to continue in sin so that grace may increase?
>
> - Romans 6:1

Paul argues against a form of this thinking where some believed that if grace always increases to cover sin, then people should not worry about increasing sin because greater sin only promoted more grace from God.

> May it never be! How shall we who died to sin still live in it?
>
> - Romans 6:2

Paul argues that those who enjoy grace do so because they have died to sin, not because they live for sin.

> As obedient children, do not be conformed to the former lusts which were yours in your ignorance, but like the Holy One who called you, be holy yourselves also in all your behavior; because it is written, "You shall be holy, for I am holy."
>
> - I Peter 1:14-16

Peter reminds Christians that God has expectations of His people and their conduct, and grace is what motivates and produces this conduct. Grace therefore is not an excuse for lukewarmness, worldliness, indifference to sin, unscriptural practices in worship, church organization, or doctrinal matters. Grace is not an excuse, on the contrary, it is a reason to be more fervent, more zealous and more careful than ever.

What is grace?

Let us look at the word and its meaning, a definition and then examine a few examples to see grace in action in people's lives.

Word meaning in the Old Testament

In the Old Testament, every instance where the word grace is used comes from a root word that means to bend or stoop. The application of this word is the bending down in kindness (as the motivation) to someone or something inferior, resulting in favors or blessings. For example, in Genesis 6:8, "Noah found favor in the eyes of the Lord."

Word meaning in the New Testament

The word translated grace in the New Testament begins at a different place but ends up meaning the same. The root word refers to a cheerful attitude. The application of the word is to express kindness (a happy heart expressing itself, favors, blessings):

- The child continued to grow and become strong, increasing in wisdom; and the grace of God was upon him. - Luke 2:40

- (Barnabas) witnessed the graoo of God - Acts 11:23

- You who are seeking to be justified by law: you have fallen from grace. - Galatians 5:4

The word always refers to a favor whether as an attitude or the result of an attitude.

Definition

The word grace refers to two things:

1. God's character. Among other things He is gracious (kind and joyful). This motivates Him to create and bless.

2. The blessings that He has given us, especially salvation by faith.

> But now apart from the Law the righteousness of God has been manifested, being witnessed by the Law and the Prophets, even the righteousness of God through faith in Jesus Christ for all those who believe; for there is no distinction; for all have sinned and fall short of the glory of God, being justified as a gift by His grace through the redemption which is in Christ Jesus;
>
> - Romans 3:21-24

Not just salvation. He could have terminated us, He could have provided salvation only through restitution (the Law). But because He is kind and joyful He provides salvation based on our association with Christ (who earned our salvation through restitution or perfect law keeping). He did it so we would not have to.

Grace, therefore, is not a line, a thermometer or a free ticket, it is a favor that God in His kindness has done for us.

By associating ourselves with Jesus through faith expressed in repentance, baptism and fidelity, we receive the same sin-free, sonship, eternal life status that He enjoys. It is a favor because there is no other way we could achieve it, it has to come from God.

Examples of grace in action

1. David and Bathsheba – II Samuel 11:1-ff

In this story King David seduces the wife of one of his military officers and the woman becomes pregnant. He then has this man killed in order to hide his sin. He lies to the nation over whom God has made him king in order to cover up the affair. By **law** he should have been condemned to death! This was the restitution necessary.

> Then David said to Nathan, "I have sinned against the Lord." And Nathan said to David, "The Lord also has taken away your sin; you shall not die.
>
> - II Samuel 12:13

David makes a simple statement to Nathan (repentance) and gets a simple reply (forgiveness). David suffered socially and emotionally as a result of his sins but God, in His grace, forgave him.

David could not give anything to God as restitution for his terrible sins, but because of His kindness, God allowed Christ to make restitution for David's sins so he would be saved spiritually and because of His kindness

He allowed David to continue as king. God did David a favor: GRACE.

2. Paul the Apostle – I Corinthians 15:9-10

Paul persecuted Christians, he broke up families, harmed and jailed innocent people. He even participated in the death of the first Christian martyr, Stephen. Many who suffered at his hands may have still been in jail or separated when he was converted, certainly nothing could compensate these people for what he did. He could not get them out of jail. What could he give to God in exchange for his sins? Not all of his mission work and suffering could bring Stephen back from the dead.

Paul understood that he was saved, he was useful only because God did him the favor of charging **all** his sins to Christ so that he could go on living. That is grace!

Summary

> When you were dead in your transgressions and the uncircumcision of your flesh, He made you alive together with Him, having forgiven us all our transgressions, having canceled out the certificate of debt consisting of decrees against us, which was hostile to us; and He has taken it out of the way, having nailed it to the cross.
>
> - Colossians 2:13-14

Paul gives us a vivid image of the working of grace on our behalf when he describes how God nails our debts (sins) to the cross so that Christ can make restitution for them by His death.

When we are worried about our salvation because we are dwelling on past sins, present weaknesses, future temptations, remember the image of the cross with our perfect Lord on it. All of our debts for sin are securely nailed to that cross. When we do this we will feel the relief that comes with this assurance.

In closing this chapter I want you to think of your worst sin, the one that causes you the greatest worry, pain and fear. Picture it as a bill or invoice and in your mind go nail it to the cross and leave it there for Jesus to make restitution for you, once and for all. Then, walk away and don't look back ever again.

CHAPTER 5
MY GRACE IS SUFFICIENT

Have you ever noticed that there is always something holding you back? Let me put it another way, have you noticed that there is always a fly in the ointment, always one or two things that prevent you from having everything you want, or having it your way?

For example:

- You have a great job, a great family but there is something wrong with your body (headaches, diabetes, sore back, etc.) that interferes with total enjoyment.

- You have just built the house you always wanted and discover that your neighbor has a constantly barking dog or a couple of noisy roosters.

- You have worked hard, saved up, gotten the children settled, you are ready to travel, but your father dies leaving you a sick mother to care for 24 hours a day.

- You are young and strong and smart but struggle with depression or a secret sin that only you know about.

I could go on but I think you get the picture. It seems that no matter what is right with our lives, there is always something that takes the shine off, something that spoils what could be an ideal situation. Of course we are not unique and this is not a new phenomenon in life. Even Paul, one of the most dynamic Apostles, experienced this type of disappointment and wrote about it.

Background

Paul the Apostle was undoubtedly one of the most successful preachers, writers, missionaries and Apostles ever to serve the church. He performed miracles. God used him to write a good portion of the New Testament. He established most of the first congregations of the church in the Roman Empire. He was responsible for breeching the wall between Jew and Gentile. All of this success and all of these blessings upon his ministry were tempered with many disappointments. For example, he was often beaten and jailed, and many, in and out of the church, opposed him. If this were not enough, several of his close associates abandoned him and the work.

It seemed that no matter what heights he scaled in the service of the Lord, there was always a spoiler, always a competing negative force making sure that the situation was never completely satisfying. This pattern finally came to a head one day when Paul was given a special vision and revelation from the Lord which literally took him out of this dimension and somehow transported him into the heavenly or spiritual realm.

Paul describes the experience in II Corinthians 12. Speaking of himself in the third person (for humility's sake), Paul says of this experience:

> Boasting is necessary, though it is not profitable; but I will go on to visions and revelations of the Lord. I know a man in Christ who fourteen years

ago—whether in the body I do not know, or out of the body I do not know, God knows—such a man was caught up to the third heaven. And I know how such a man—whether in the body or apart from the body I do not know, God knows was caught up into Paradise and heard inexpressible words, which a man is not permitted to speak.

- II Corinthians 12:1-4

Imagine the feeling and the absolute thrill of being brought into the heavenly realm while still in this earthly body. Imagine the joy, the sense of empowerment, the gratitude, the zeal and renewed faith this could give a person.

If Paul was a mighty preacher and teacher, if he was a zealous missionary before this experience, imagine what he could be after such a vision! What a spiritual boost - to consciously see and experience heaven before you die! Now, just as he is spiritually pumped, spiritually invincible because of this vision, look at what happens, see what he says comes along immediately after his mountaintop experience.

Because of the surpassing greatness of the revelations, for this reason, to keep me from exalting myself, there was given me a thorn in the flesh, a messenger of Satan to torment me—to keep me from exalting myself!

- II Corinthians 12:7

No sooner than he was at the top, a thorn, a restriction, a spoiler, a downer was added to the mix. There is a lot of discussion about what exactly happened (vision problems, disease, etc.) but who cares what it was. The point that Paul makes is that for him it was a burden, a restriction, a spoiler, a thorn as he refers to it. Something that caused pain and diverted his attention from the sublime experience he had planned to enjoy to a discomforting annoyance always present.

This is where Christians part company with the rest of the world. For unbelievers, when there is a problem, the objective is to minimize and eliminate the thorns as quickly and painlessly as possible. For unbelievers the ultimate goal is personal happiness and freedom from "thorns." Christians, on the other hand, have a different approach, one articulated by Paul in his effort to deal with his particular thorn.

He mentions three possible responses for the "spoiler" elements and "thorns" that often come into our lives to threaten our peace, happiness and contentment.

1. Prayer

> Concerning this I implored the Lord three times that it might leave me.
>
> - II Corinthians 12:8

Paul prayed a legitimate prayer that the thorn be removed. Notice also that he kept on praying until he had some kind of relief or response! Simply resigning ourselves to difficulties, obstacles and the "thorns" of life is not necessarily the Christian thing to do. It is okay to aggressively seek to remove the things that reduce our joy, our satisfaction of life, as well as our peace and happiness.

- If there is a cure, I want it.
- If there is a solution, I want it.
- If there is a way out, show me.

Having exhausted his natural resources in dealing with the problem Paul began to beat on the door of heaven through prayer for relief. Prayer is an effective tool in removing the many thorns of life that often spoil what could be a good life. Sometimes our prayers for relief are answered and we simply continue on in the way we were before our thorn began to cause us pain. Sometimes our prayers for relief are answered, but not in the way we had hoped, and sometimes God chooses to leave the thorn in place for an indefinite amount of time. In these cases we have another response which Paul describes in verse 9.

2. Submission

> And He has said to me, "My grace is sufficient for you, for power is perfected in weakness." Most gladly, therefore, I will rather boast about my weaknesses, so that the power of Christ may dwell in me.
>
> - II Corinthians 12:9

In this verse God speaks to Paul and Paul responds to the Lord. God's answer to his prayers is to remind Paul of the spiritual principle that the thorn has been sent to teach him: that God's power is more easily and clearly seen in a person who is weak and dependent on God than one who is strong and self-sufficient.

It would be easy for Paul, the miracle worker, the prolific missionary and the insightful teacher to stumble into pride and conceit on account of all his incredible achievements. It would be easy for the church to exalt the man Paul for his abilities and success above other men. But this thorn reduced him to dependence on others to do his work; this thorn drove him to his knees in prayer for strength.

And so, despite his great success and prestige in the church, this thorn served to reveal the true source of his power in ministry; this thorn was a constant reminder that his was a fragile life held delicately in the hand of God. You see, Paul's submission was not necessarily a submission to the presence of the thorn (that's the best that unbelievers can do when they have a thorn that will not go away, simply accept its constant presence and carry on). That is stoicism!

No, Paul's submission was to the purpose that God had for allowing it to enter and remain in his life. This is what he says when he answers the Lord. He submits to the change in circumstances and the shift that his life has taken because of the thorn. He's gone from being a strong and independent man to a physically weak and dependent one and he submits to God's new demand of him.

The new demand is that he witness Christ through his weakness rather than through his former strength. Rather than be depressed, angry or refuse to accept the new reality, Paul sees the opportunity to reveal

Christ in a way that he could not before: through his weakness. And so, as Christians we submit to the thorns of life by learning to glorify God and serve Christ as people with thorns. Do you see the difference? Some people simply learn to live with their thorns and make the best of it. Christians, like Paul, are called upon to glorify God despite the thorn.

3. Rise Above

> Therefore I am well content with weaknesses, with insults, with distresses, with persecutions, with difficulties, for Christ's sake; for when I am weak, then I am strong.
>
> - II Corinthians 12:10

When I say, "rise above," I do not mean to ignore the problem; pretend it does not exist; try to be as much like a person without a thorn as I can be. Look at what Paul says:

- He is well content with weakness, the particular thorn he prayed about.

- He is also well content with all the other "thorns" he has had to suffer as well (insults, distress, persecution etc.).

- He acknowledges that he is a man with many thorns and yet he is content - wait a minute!

Is contentment not what we are looking for? Is contentment not what we think we will find when we remove all the thorns, all the restraints and all the spoilers? He goes on to acknowledge that to bear with the thorns for Christ's sake, to be made weak for Christ's sake, makes him strong.

So this man with many thorns finds contentment and strength, the same thing that people are searching for by trying to remove all the thorns of life. What is the point, what is the difference?

Enduring the thorns for Christ sake (with and for one's faith in Jesus) gives you the same thing (contentment and strength) that removing all the thorns is supposed to give you. The only difference is that you can never remove all the thorns; they are always there one way or another. And so, for a Christian, to submit to the thorns of life that God chooses to leave in your flesh, in your life is really the way to rise above the ordinary pursuit of happiness and power, and gain for oneself contentment and true strength through Christ Jesus.

So the weaker I become, the stronger Christ becomes in me. The less of me that I am, the more of Him becomes visible. The poorer I am in this world, the richer I become in Christ. The thornier my life becomes, the greater my dependence and consequently my contentment in Christ. They say, "Everybody wants to go to heaven but nobody wants to die." In the same way it seems, "Everyone wants more of Jesus in their lives but nobody wants the thorns that will bring Him to us."

Summary

We do not always realize it but God's answer to Paul's prayer is still very much the answer to our own daily prayers concerning the various "thorns" we struggle with. When we apply these words to ourselves we see that, God's grace is truly sufficient in every way now as it was then:

1. His grace is still sufficient to supply our needs.

Whether it is food, shelter or help with troubles and sickness, God still supplies according to His grace, which is boundless. There is no need to trust in worldly riches or the power of man, God's grace is able to supply our every need; we need only to ask, believing (Matthew 6:25-34).

2. His Grace is still sufficient to cover our sins.

Jesus died once for all people and all sins (I John 1:9-10). When coming to God for forgiveness realize that His grace covers every sin you have committed, there is no need to fear or worry.

3. His Grace is still sufficient to complete our final transformation.

What the Law could not accomplish, the grace of Christ completes in full (Romans 8:3-4). Our final resurrection to glory and exaltation to the right hand of God is powered by grace and there is sufficient grace to transform every believer into an eternal being. Paul the Apostle learned that what he needed was not relief or more strength but rather the realization that if he had God's grace, he had all he would ever need to achieve all he ever really desired.

Do you have God's grace working in your life? It begins to work in you when you submit to His command to believe in Jesus Christ, repent of your sins and be united with Him in the waters of baptism. It continues to work in you as you submit to God's plan for your life, whatever that is, however many thorns that may include. It completes its work when Jesus returns for you in death or glory for the final and eternal transformation.

CHAPTER 6
THE IMPACT OF GRACE

People's lives are changed or impacted by many things good and bad. I remember as a 15-year-old boy in Montreal, my mother coming into my room in the middle of the night to tell me my father was dying. He had been well, I had seen him alive before I went to bed that evening and now a few hours later, he lay dead in his room, the victim of a sudden heart attack at 53 years of age. That event impacted my life in many ways, and changed its direction for a long period of time.

Fifteen years later, when I was around 30, I remember sending this girl I knew a postcard. We had been friends and I had not seen her for a couple of years because she had moved to France and I remained in Canada. One Christmas, I decided to send her a postcard in order to say hello. What I did not know was that during the few years I had not seen or heard from her, this girl had left Paris and moved back to Montreal. That little postcard went from Montreal to Paris and when it got there the building janitor where the girl used to live sent it back to Canada where the girl had moved to. When she received the postcard forwarded from France she looked me up and about a year later that girl, Lise, and I were married. We still have the postcard in our scrapbook. That small act of sending a greeting to a girl I once knew had a tremendous and wonderful impact on my life.

I tell these stories from my own life to underscore the idea that there are certain events or people that have a lasting impact on our lives. Not every event or person, but some events and some people come into our lives and change them forever. I would like to build on this idea and explain to you how one's life is changed when it is impacted by the grace of God.

The Bible is filled with all kinds of information and stories about God, His chosen people, the coming of Jesus and the establishment of the Church. What the Bible is about, however, is God's effort to impart His grace to every person through Christ. Yes, there are descriptions of the creation, lessons about faith, teachings from Christ and His Apostles, but when you bring all of the information together, what the Bible ultimately gives us is the incredible story of God's love for man and how that love/grace changes or impacts a person's life for good.

Obviously I do not have the time or ability to detail every change brought on by God's grace, but I can give you three main ones that represent, in one way or another, most of the others. Three ways that the impact of God's grace changes our lives:

1. Grace makes us eager to obey.

The worldly person celebrates and applauds disobedience and rebellion. Just look at our heroes. They are the ones who break the rules, bend the rules or make their own rules in order to get what they want. However, when people come into contact with the grace of God, they are the ones who are broken and humbled.

Jesus describes the feeling when He says,

> Blessed are those who hunger and thirst for righteousness for they will be satisfied.
>
> - Matthew 5:6

It is a hunger, a thirst, a constant desire to know what is right and do what is right. John nails the experience when he says,

> No one who abides in Him sins, no one who sins has seen Him or knows Him.
>
> - I John 3:6

Some think John is saying that Christians never sin, never make a mistake and never fall. We know from experience that this is not true. John's point is that those who have been impacted by God's grace do not want to sin, their spirits yearn for purity and righteousness. Those who know Him cannot practice sin. On the contrary, they want the very opposite which is to quit sinning and practice obedience. No law, no meditation, no exercise, philosophy or book can make you want to obey.

This desire is the result of God's grace and because of it our character, our actions and the directions in our lives are changed forever.

2. Grace makes us work hard.

I am not saying that anyone who works hard has been impacted by grace. Many people work hard for various reasons. Some work hard to care for families. Some work hard to get ahead or get rich. And some work hard because they like to work or they have a dream to accomplish something.

But those who have been impacted by grace work hard in an area where these others would not invest a minute, and that is in the building up of the kingdom of God here on earth, what we call the church. Paul describes this labor of love brought upon him by God's grace.

> For I am the least of the apostles, and not fit to be called an apostle, because I persecuted the church of God. But by the grace of God I am what I am, and His grace toward me did not prove vain; but I labored even more than all of them, yet not I, but the grace of God with me.
>
> - I Corinthians 15:9-10

A little further on Paul describes the effort and suffering he has endured because of God's grace.

> Are they servants of Christ? I speak as if insane — I more so; in far more labors, in far more imprisonments, beaten times without number, often in danger of death. Five times I received from the Jews thirty-nine lashes. Three times I was beaten with rods, once I was stoned, three times I was shipwrecked, a night and a day I have spent in the deep. I have been on frequent journeys, in dangers from rivers, dangers from robbers, dangers from my countrymen, dangers from the Gentiles, dangers in the city, dangers in the wilderness, dangers on the sea, dangers

among false brethren; I have been in labor and hardship, through many sleepless nights, in hunger and thirst, often without food, in cold and exposure. Apart from such external things, there is the daily pressure on me of concern for all the churches.

- II Corinthians 11:23-28

Note that in this passage Paul does not even mention the thousands of miles traveled, the lessons and sermons given, the epistles written and the men trained, not to mention his ministry to the poor and the ill. What would move a man who was a religious leader with a comfortable position and a bright future to abandon it all and earn his living as a tradesman from day to day and endure such a difficult and demanding life?

Paul said it back in I Corinthians 15:10

By the grace of God, I am what I am.

You know, I can always tell the difference between those people who have been educated in the doctrine of grace and those who have truly experienced the power of God's grace in their lives.

A. Those who have been indoctrinated know the church traditions and can spout the Christian lingo, but there's no "fire in the belly." They don't volunteer, they don't try to know or help others and they are not usually generous when it comes to giving. They think that Christianity is about coming to church on Sundays.

They do not realize that attending worship is not serving the Lord; worship and Bible study are times when the Lord is serving us through His word and Spirit.

B. Those who have truly been impacted by God's grace, on the other hand show it by their desire to serve, work, give and sacrifice. These brethren may not say much but their work and their contribution say it all, to the world, to the Church and to the Lord. Jesus said that those who are forgiven little, love little and those who are forgiven much, love much (Luke 7:47).

Perhaps this is what separates the men from the boys when it comes to hard work in the name of the Lord. Perhaps people who are less motivated are that way because they don't realize what kind of sorry sinners they really are and figure they don't owe God a lot, and those who bear the heat of the day and the sweat of heavy spiritual lifting know themselves a little better.

Maybe it is a question of personal honesty and self-awareness. All I know is that those who are painfully aware of their true condition before God are usually the most productive, and those who are spiritually nearsighted don't usually generate much horsepower. Did Paul the Apostle not say, "I am the chief of sinners."? Maybe that is the connection between grace and the desire to work hard for the Lord.

3. Grace makes us thankful.

No other gift given to us in life is more precious than the grace of God, because the Bible says:

- It is by grace that Jesus was sent to die for our sins - Hebrews 2:9

- It is by grace that the world came to know about Christ - Titus 2:11

- It is by grace that we personally have received the truth - John 1:17

- It is by grace that we are saved - Acts 15:11

- It is by grace that we are justified/forgiven of sins - Romans 3:24

- It is by grace that we receive the promise of God - Romans 4:16

- It is by grace that we enjoy peace with God - Romans 5:2

- It is by grace that we are made free from the demands of the Law - Romans 6:14

- It is by grace that we have hope for the future - II Thessalonians 2:16

Are you getting a feel for how precious God's grace or favor is?

- It is by grace that we become who we are in Christ - I Corinthians 15 :10

- It is by grace that we receive gifts so we can minister to others - Romans12:6

- It is by grace that we have the courage to speak out
  - Romans 15:15

- It is by grace that we are able:

  o To give thanks - II Corinthians 4:15

  o To give joyful praise - Colossians 3:16

  o To go boldly before God in prayer - Hebrews 4:16

- It is by grace that we have, each day, what we need when we need it - Hebrews 4:16

- Finally, it is by grace that we are perfected, confirmed, strengthened and established so we can live forever with God in Christ. - I Peter 5:10

Because of these and all other blessings showered down upon us by grace, our hearts are turned to gratitude. A life impacted by grace finds a reason to give thanks in everything seen, heard and felt. For this reason Paul says to Titus that grace,

> ...teaches us to say no to ungodliness, passion, to live upright and Godly lives...
>
> - Titus 2:11-12

Eventually just saying thank you is not enough, the feeling of gratitude spills out in to joyful praise, holy and dedicated living and a genuine love for this grace. In speaking of God's grace in terms of the kingdom, the Hebrew writer summarizes it best when he says,

> Therefore since we receive a kingdom which cannot be shaken, let us show gratitude, by which we may offer to God an acceptable service with reverence and awe.
>
> - Hebrews12:28

The single most recognizable characteristic in the lives of those who have been impacted by the grace of God is a thankful and appreciative heart. Whether times are good or bad these brethren are always sensitive to and grateful for God's grace in Christ Jesus.

Summary

Let us bring this discussion home. Ask yourself, has the grace of God had an impact on my life?

Let me help you answer that question:

1. Grace has impacted your life if doing what the Lord wants you to do is continually growing in importance in your life. In other words, you may not be perfect but you would like to be! And getting rid of sin is a joyful event not a sad nostalgic one.

2. Grace has impacted your life if more of your time and resources have been devoted to the Lord this year than last year. Sure we get sick or busy, but in all honesty, is the time, effort and money you are investing in the Lord and His Church growing or shrinking?

Note that Paul's life and ministry was not meant to be a monument or a one-time thing. It was meant to be an example for us to follow! He said to imitate him as He imitated Christ. Jesus did what He did because He wanted to give us grace; Paul did what he did because he received grace. The question is, "What do we have to show for the grace that's come into our lives?"

3. Grace has impacted your life if much of your prayer life and much of the motivation for what you do is based on gratitude. The virtue of being grateful is the first one to be cultivated in order to be pleasing to God. Oh, we can be weak in many areas, struggling with bad habits and sinful actions, but if we can begin to be grateful for God's kindness and grace, all of these other things can be conquered. In Romans 1:21, Paul says that an ungrateful heart is the first sin that sends man heading into the darkness of every other sin.

BibleTalk.tv is an Internet Mission Work.

We provide textual Bible teaching material on our website and mobile apps for free. We enable churches and individuals all over the world to have access to high quality Bible materials for personal growth, group study or for teaching in their classes.

The goal of this mission work is to spread the gospel to the greatest number of people using the latest technology available. For the first time in history it is becoming possible to preach the gospel to the entire world at once. BibleTalk.tv is an effort to preach the gospel to all nations every day until Jesus returns.

The Choctaw Church of Christ in Oklahoma City is the sponsoring congregation for this work and provides the recording facilities and oversight. If you wish to support this work please contact us at the address below.

choctawsaints.org/support-bibletalk

Made in the USA
Lexington, KY
06 July 2017